Stronger Than Cleopatra

Poems By
Jacqueline Jules

Copyright © 2014 Jacqueline Jules
Copyright © 2014 Cover Art by Alan Hechtkopf

ELJ Publications, LLC ~ New York
ELJ Publications Series

All rights reserved.

ISBN: 978-1-941617
ISBN 13: 978-1-941617-03-8

for Bill, Seventeen Years Together

CONTENTS

Yellow Marigolds	3
The Words We Did Not Speak	4
911	5
Call a Friend	6
First Grief	7
Four Days After Your Funeral	8
Sweet Dreams	9
The Old Woman in the Grocery Store	10
The Scarecrow	11
On My Right Hand	13
The Blue Dress	14
Empty Spaces	15
Grocery Shopping	16
Five Months	17
Shadow	18
Birthday Gifts	19
Shoes	20
Worms in the Flour	22
Stronger Than Cleopatra	24
Balm	25
The Last Night in this House	26
Giggle	28
This Side of the River	29
Tail	30
Sirens	31
Empty Bed	32
Second Time	33
Wings from a Chrysalis	35
Anniversary	36
Banquet Hall Collapse	38

ACKNOWLEDGMENTS

Several poems in this collection have been published in the following journals in various forms:

Animus, Chiron Review, Cider Press Review, Connecticut River Review, Holiday Hope, Jewish Women's Literary Annual, The Journal of Poetry Therapy, Lines + Stars, Lullwater Review, The Main Street Rag, Minimus, Mobius, Potpourri, Scapegoat Review, Sow's Ear Poetry Review, St. Anthony Messenger, Sunstone, Timber Creek Review, Verve

Yellow Marigolds

Rising up from the ground,
yellow faces tilted toward the sun.
I planted them after the house was sold,
for the new owners to enjoy.
Silly, I suppose
to invest time and money
in something else I had to leave behind.
Yet, pulling out of the driveway
that last time,
I enjoyed those yellow blooms,
planted yearly in the same spot.
They stood in front of the yard,
in front of the story
the neighbors would tell
of a long red fire truck
lumbering at the curb,
two men with medical bags
emerging from red doors,
and a small brown-haired wife
standing barefoot on the steps
waving both arms and screaming,
"Hurry! Hurry! Hurry!"
when it was already too late.

The Words We Did Not Speak

I woke early without remorse;
ready to tackle the tasks
taunting yesterday and the day before.
Sitting up in our bed,
I did not pause
to kiss your peaceful face
but moved to the list
I planned to check off before sunset.
You were on the second list—
end-of-the-day extras if
energy endured.

Midmorning, the house was still quiet.
All awake but self-absorbed. Love
we could have expressed (had we known)
hummed like a ceiling fan,
maintaining comfort, unnoticed.

The boys say they ate cold cereal with you
before running to the rec room and Nintendo.
On my way to the kitchen, I saw you in the den,
still in green paisley pajamas, pencil and papers in hand.
If you looked pale, I did not notice.

A quiet morning. I can't remember
if we touched or even if we smiled.
But now, every moment feels the silence
of our last hours together
and the words we did not speak.

911

Disbelief. My only thought
as I blew in your mouth
and our son pounded your chest.
Disbelief.
Your eyes were white
when I lifted the lids;
your cheeks purple.
Disbelief.
I heard sirens and ran down the hall.
Our son screamed—
a megaphone against my ear.
His repeated cries accused us both
of leaving a thirteen-year-old boy
alone.
Two men came.
I opened the door,
pointed, and ran back down the hall.
Our son rose as the paramedics kneeled.
A policeman appeared,
politely pushed us out of the way.
In silence, we watched
the stretcher rattle
through the front door.
I stood erect,
as stiff as your rigid body.
My right hand, then my left
miming the oxygen mask on your face.
Every second exhaled
the breath
we wanted restored
to you.

Call a Friend

It was decided in the patrol car,
with the blond policeman.
He looked about forty, a father I presumed,
the kind of man who might coach Little League
in the same voice he used with me.
Call someone to meet you.

At the house, he had kept me busy with questions:
Who is your husband's doctor? What medications did he take?
I scurried back and forth presenting slips
of useless information he funneled to the paramedics
as he calmly directed the show,
an episode of Twilight Zone in black and white.
Call a neighbor to take your kids.
We'll follow the ambulance in my car.

Like a battered wife afraid of more bruises,
I obeyed in silence until he ordered me to call a friend.
Someone should be with you.
No. Michelle is busy. So are Jeanne, Leslie, Carol.
Skillfully, he struck down each excuse until
it was a fly flattened beneath a swatter.
You shouldn't be alone.

So Debbie was called on the police radio. Static punctuated
the request which hurried her to the hospital
to hold my hand
as the doctor confirmed
what I knew was true
from the moment
I was told
to call a friend.

First Grief

The gasp was hers,
not mine.
My mouth was covered,
clamping the sound
I did not make—
a whoosh
like a truck speeding past in the rain
spraying a puddle on our cheeks.

A Good Samaritan on the scene,
Debbie had accompanied me
to a tidy hospital office
with blond wood furniture
and red-speckled seats
to watch the dark-haired doctor
shake his head.
Her body stiffened
as mine crumpled
beneath the sound
escaping from her lips.

Like the survivors of Auschwitz
who first saw their skeletal shape
in the tears of the soldiers who saved them—
my grief opened in that gasp.

Four Days After Your Funeral

Thunder wakes me.
It is Sunday morning. 3 a.m.
The sound is a giant stamping his foot,
pulling trees out of the ground,
ripping rocks from a mountainside.
It is clearly a temper tantrum, clearly you,
and I sit up in bed to listen.
Your anger explodes over the roof,
fuels the wind, banging
on the window, blowing out the lights.
I hug my knees in the dark as you howl
and howl
until my own rage rises
to the sky beside you. Together,
we hurl stones at the earth below—
a team of two-year-olds
demanding repair of a toy
irreparably broken.
But it feels good,
one last time,
to cry together.

Sweet Dreams

Am I sleeping?
A positive answer shocks.
People assume insomnia,
restless strength
to toss from side to side,
get up for tea or hot milk.
No, I love the dark,
the cool embrace of the bed,
a burrow of refuge, hibernation.
In the dark, I hear the floor creak
under your feet, feel the weight
of your body entering. . . .

In the dark, you are not dead.

Dawn spews a rosy mist
the morning light annihilates.
Then tears make the sheets
cold and too heavy to lift.
My limbs are wood,
rotting in a damp forest.
The air reeks of sweet dreams
I must forget.

The Old Woman in the Grocery Store

At 38 years, I fear old age:
not wrinkles or white hair,
not even senility.
It's the odds I object to.
Additional years multiply chances
of standing at a grave site
shoveling dirt on a life I love.
Growing old means outlasting others,
a most unappealing idea
after the summer afternoon
pool plans were suddenly scrapped
for a meeting with the undertaker.
Do you have a picture we can run with the obit?
Should the service be indoors or out?
Life is too brittle; too much like old bones
that snap in the slightest fall.
I hold my breath
at the sight of someone
who has survived the years.
She is standing by the meat counter,
thin, white-haired, with blue-veined fingers
stubbornly grasping a grocery cart.
I can't help but stare—as if watching
a movie star choose ground beef.

The Scarecrow

I used to complain about our social life.
Moving three times to new cities,
we didn't have enough friends,
or so I thought until the morning you died
and the phone rang and rang.
People call, and we discuss the boys,
my job, the schools, the weather—everything
but why they think of me so often.
I am the widow now,
the scarecrow on a suburban lawn—
like our neighbor back in Pittsburgh,
widowed by a frightened deer.

Remember how we sent away
for those silly plastic whistles?
Attached them to the front bumper,
charms to ward off sudden silent creatures
that crash through windshields on dark winding roads. . . .

I wonder how many neighbors and friends
saw cardiologists in the weeks
after your funeral. Curiosity, not criticism.
Do others feel what I did in Pittsburgh,
months after the deer accident, seeing the widow
shopping in the mall, buying clothes for a son
still growing despite his father's death?
I was transfixed by the sight—
the widow standing up—
not propped and bound to a pole.
Standing up, admitting good days and bad days,

while adjusting a battered hat and
pushing straw back into an old plaid shirt.
Standing up. On her own. Standing up.

On My Right Hand

You were buried
with your wedding ring.
"Not what we usually do,"
the funeral director complained.
But your ring
wasn't a problem. Mine was.
After 17 years, my third finger
was shriveled at the base,
dented with a white circle
like pile carpet under a couch.
I felt exposed, leaving the house
with naked hands.
But gold on my left hand,
signifying wife,
was as hot as candy
swiped from a store counter.
A dilemma each time I dressed,
until a gentle friend suggested
my right hand—
where my rings
could remain,
like yours,
forever.

The Blue Dress

Black wasn't necessary
as long as it was dark, they said.
I only felt relief
when the designated friend
emerged from my closet
declaring no need to shop:
I could wear the blue dress,
the one I'd worn to job interviews,
professional meetings, dinner engagements.
My all-purpose yet classy blue dress,
just fine for your funeral,
with black shoes and black hat.
The buttons in the back
were hard to fasten by myself
but I managed that morning
and this one.
It feels odd, of course,
wearing clothes I wore to say goodbye.
I could have wrapped this dress in plastic,
stored it with my wedding gown,
as if designed for a single solemn occasion.
I won't.
There's no need to discard
everything I loved in my life before.

Empty Spaces

Single or double?
The question hurled me
across the room
like a rag doll,
limp, unable to respond.
Irreversible decision, the rabbi counseled,
the second plot can be sold,
not purchased later.
If I want a space beside you—
thirty, forty years from now,
a plot must be waiting
so you won't be alone forever
the way I am now,
too young to leave the children,
the way you did,
and fill the space
I did not leave beside you—
refusing to reserve
more empty spaces in my life.

Grocery Shopping

If you are watching me now
above these fluorescent lights,
you'd be pleased to see me pause
over prices touted as super.
Your voice is alive in my head,
as I reconsider complaints
over unclipped coupons, bargains I missed.
I remember us as newlyweds
arguing at the meat counter:
cuts of beef bored me, I didn't care for red meat.
Would you have been happier
with a wife who read the weekly ads,
someone who shared your passion for specials?
Such a wife wouldn't have disappointed you
as often as I did,
especially in the first years
when I peeled price tags off purchases,
not having your patience to wait for sales.
In the aisles alone now,
the cart is so heavy pushing past
the items you would have liked.
The wheels squeak
with the sound of your sighs
when we fought.
It feels as if you were always angry with me,
as I am with myself
for wasting time those final minutes,
calling your name and asking questions,
"Can you hear me? Should I call 911?"
Can you hear me—
Now?

Five Months

I can drive home from work now
without dripping on the steering wheel,
wailing my request
for the window they say pops open
with every closed door.
No longer ceaselessly submerged
I can grab the handle,
roll down the glass
and escape to the surface
where my lungs fill
without panic or pain
for two or three days at a time.
Should I be ashamed
if others see me smiling?
Five months—
too soon
for recovery,
too long for public tears.
I don't know
what to expect
from myself or others.
When I'm in control,
capable of driving sanely,
the guard rail gleams in the sunlight,
signaling danger in the curves to come.

Shadow

Children play with their shadows,
shouting, "You can't catch me!"
They laugh at long dark fingers
mimicking every move.

While I see a silhouette
on the sidewalk
and sob.

The day of your death
is attached to my life
as securely as shadow
stretching from my heels
in the bright morning sun.
A stubborn companion,
standing behind and beyond.

It watches me.

Daring me to dance in the light.

Birthday Gifts

A man who reads a woman's mind
is a greeting card fantasy,
invented by someone who lives alone.
Only single people don't quarrel
over who took out the trash last,
who left the lights on,
who didn't put the ketchup in the fridge.
Small clashes coat cohabitation
like grease on a fry pan.
Too often, we forgot to watch the stove
and black smoke covered the walls.
If I wanted carrot cake,
not chocolate;
a bracelet, not a blender—
I could have told you
before my birthday arrived.
Now, when your life has been
etched on a stone with two dates,
it's too late to say
I should have opened
more of your gifts with delight.

Shoes

In an outlet store in New England
on a trip two years ago,
you bought nine pairs of your favorite shoes.
We laughed then, a nine year supply
lugged in suitcases across seven states.
Such belief we had in the future;
to plan footwear seven years beyond your death.
Yet the pleasure in your smile remains:
Super price! Super fit! Super comfortable!
I feigned chagrin over the
logistics of carrying so many shoes on the plane,
then bought three pairs myself.
Life has so many mundane moments,
meaningful in retrospect.
The image is more vivid than the
photographs on the wall:
my low-key husband,
vivacious that day,
on vacation, willing to splurge.

A sense of duty
to others less fortunate
has donated a dead man's suits, shirts, ties, belts,
but your shoes remain, size 13 B width,
empty, in the back of the closet.
Can I let someone else wear your shoes?
Enjoy the comfortable fit the way you did?
A delicate subject I didn't consider in the first grim days
when all I could see was you, on your back,
unconscious, convulsing, the pain in your body

pulling you away before there was time
to cry and plead: Don't go! Don't go! Don't
leave me with all these shoes.

Worms in the Flour

The sweet smell of baking bread
widened your nostrils, then your eyes.
"A girl who bakes bread!" Your face,
a nomad finding water in the desert.
It was the seventies.
Men were afraid to open doors, afraid not to.
You were ten years my senior.
"Challah," I corrected. "Sabbath bread.
An expression of faith."

When time allows and mood demands,
I still set out bowls and measuring cups,
yeast, eggs, and flour on the kitchen counter,
determined to knead a sticky white mess
into something smooth and solid.
It's a noisy process. The first time
you heard the sound
of something being punched and beaten,
you ran to the kitchen to watch.

It requires more strength now,
in the house alone.
Finding the cabinet empty of yeast,
I can't ask you to put down the newspaper
and run to the store. I almost quit today—
opening the flour tin, finding worms.

But there were empty bowls
on the counter, waiting
beside sugar, yeast, and eggs.

They taunted me, dared me to continue.
I grabbed my coat and keys.

Not long after, I came back
with new flour, ready
to start over.

Stronger Than Cleopatra

Colleagues comment,
one even complained
that I've been silent.
Smiling all day with my students
as if grief was as foreign as Egypt.
No conscious plan to be a sphinx,
I am grateful for young faces
asking questions,
reminders of a world beyond
one widowed teacher's tears.
Especially today,
as we consider Cleopatra
and her choice to follow Antony,
who threw himself on his sword too soon.
I understand what it means
to be imprisoned by grief.
with my ships burned and armies destroyed.
I want to test poisons, too.
But the clear, young eyes before me
suggest I can be stronger than Cleopatra.
That I can dress in my finest robes
and enjoy what is left of the figs
without the poison asp.

Balm

His touch is a poultice
applied to aching, inflamed skin.
My back, flayed open by grief,
screams for the balm of his hands.
You didn't leave me scarred
by angry nights
recoiled at the edge of the bed.
You left me
accustomed to closeness.
Suddenly bereft of the man
who cuddled me to sleep every night,
my body burned like a suttee,
except I survived—
to kiss another.
Loss made me lustful,
ignited my need to love.
In his arms,
I leave the funeral pyre,
lips tasting of smoke,
grateful
he doesn't mind.

The Last Night in This House

The pictures in the hallway have been taken down
packed in mirror cartons marked fragile. In the new house,
your smile will decorate our lives without stabbing me
on a solitary walk to an empty bed.

At the end of the hall, two pink Tiffany lamps
intensify the pink in the flowers on the walls.
With only one curtained window,
it's as dim as a movie theater.
The pink flowers fade into a giant screen
showing the same film all day, all night,
as the gurney rattles through the room.

In the bathroom, I can see you alive,
lathering your face over the sink,
gliding a blue plastic razor under your chin.
The gilded mirror remembers everything,
my yellow gloved hands
cleaning furiously
four weeks after your funeral; the moment
I tossed your toothbrush and razor in the trash.

Every wall in this house emits your absence.
I choke on the fumes, every evening,
driving a single car into a double garage; every morning,
choosing dresses in a closet emptied of your suits.

The furniture, I hope, is harmless. Your brown easy chair
will be wrapped in plastic to travel on a truck beside
seventeen years of items selected together. New surroundings
won't make the blue sofa brighter,
the light wood coffee table less scratched.

But maybe I can breathe in a house where your death
is more carefully placed. Like a china figurine
behind glass in one corner of one room.

Giggle

His giggle was like a small silver bell
rolling down a flight of stairs.
The sound would somersault
in the air, head over heels,
head over heels, unable to stop.
The rest of us would pause to gaze
at his small red mouth, agape.
He was a quiet second child,
who posed few questions.
Like his father,
he didn't need words
to prove his existence.
The giggle was his hallmark,
often the only evidence
he was with us in the car or
at the dinner table.
But at age nine, the giggle
was silenced—
swallowed by the siren
that took Daddy away.
A year passed before I heard
his distinctive bell
bounce down the stairs again.
My heart did somersaults, unable to stop.

This Side of the River

Like a razor blade
slicing a striped plastic straw,
my life became two pieces, she said
before and after,
the twins born at 32 weeks
did not learn to breathe.
She chopped the air
with her right hand,
demonstrating separation
from the prior person
who had not buried babies.
I nodded and reached for her,
touching instead, the opaque screen,
between my present self
and the woman never widowed.
We cannot cross the river again;
cannot skip on the sweet new grass
that grows on the virgin side.
This side of the river is buried by lava.
We walk lightly on scorched feet.

Tail

Put it behind you, she scolds.
I have.
Can't she see my tail?
long as a monkey's
lively as a cat's,
it pokes through my skirt,
fretfully waving,
a moving appendage, indicative of mood.
No use covering it with a jacket,
just creates a wriggling hump.
Behind me:
17 years of marriage finished in a funeral.
Behind me:
the reason I moved, why my children
call my husband by his first name.
Not unusual—
who would suspect death not divorce?
if not for my sinuous tail
dancing behind me like a charmed snake
begging the question or comment
that grants permission to repeat
all the details of a death
I should put behind me,
she scolds
every time I open my mouth.

Sirens

He smiles and waves as I drive away,
and the thought rushes out
like an air bag in a crash.
Should the moment be freeze-framed
as the last smile we exchanged?
I'm always hearing sirens,
some real, some imagined,
racing toward the hospital,
and a doctor who shakes his head
and says "I'm sorry."
Six months with a shiny new ring,
and the word "husband" has
still not been disengaged from "deceased."
A siren wails and I see myself
standing at the cemetery,
this time not stoically silent, this time
screaming wildly, arms flailing,
demanding a different world,
a mythical one—without sirens,
where I can drive serenely,
knowing all accidents are behind me
and the road ahead is clear.

Empty Bed

Alone in bed, his absence
lies besides yours. The mattress
feels as large as Alaska
and no less cold.

I am a widow again,
restlessly waiting for dawn,
not a second wife waiting for
a second husband
to finish his crossword,
flush and brush.

Each night,
I stroke his shoulder,
the way I touched my newborns.
My fingers tingle.
This joy was born of blood.

Second Time

I was surprised
when my second pregnancy
was easier than my first.
The doctor, the books, my friends
all said this was normal.
Some babies kick, others snooze;
each child is unique
inside and outside the womb.
Yet sometimes, I still felt guilty
cuddling my second,
worried I hadn't treasured
each moment with my first,
that new mother fears
had frustrated the bliss
I felt the second time,
when experience eased anxiety
over burping and diapers—
the details we fret the first time.
If my second baby heard more songs
and played more pat-a-cake,
it is because he had a different mother.
The past gives the present
all new props;
I wasn't the same the second time,
not with my newborns—
not with my men.

You were my first.
We fought over how to make the bed;
on which side the clock radio should sit.
We knew togetherness, not loss.
Like the crying infant

I couldn't imagine older,
we held each other without urgency,
foolishly trusting tomorrow
to offer the loved ones of today.

Wings from a Chrysalis

I still find things when I clean closets,
like the speckled tan tie you wore to our wedding.
It has a stain. Champagne, perhaps?
We drank that day—like all young couples—
to a future we didn't expect to spill
after seventeen years
on a rose-colored carpet in the middle of June.

Who would I be had I not buried you?
The question itches sometimes
like a coarse spot on otherwise smooth skin
as I snuggle with your replacement
in a bed bigger than the one we shared. . . .

Your death reduced me to larva.
But time inside a chrysalis
gave me wings I would not give back.
I loved my old body,
but this one suits me, too,
and some creatures are destined
to live their lives in stages,
each one distinct and beautiful
while it lasts.

Anniversary

Eight years after
the seven-day candle in the tall red glass,
I light a small candle
and consider your existence
in a realm beyond my knowledge.
If life on earth is only one stage in a series,
you could be safe in an ethereal cocoon,
preparing to emerge with splendid wings in Eden.
I'm ashamed to say
your transformation into something better
brought little comfort to me in the beginning,
as I decried my status as a caterpillar,
a frightened worm, vulnerable to a large and hungry bird.

Living without you
was never as difficult
as living with your death.
The burial of a face
that still smiles at me in photographs
seemed, at times, slightly less credible
than spaceships landing on my lawn.
If I believed in death before,
it was the same way I believed in another universe
and other life forms—somewhere out there—
I wasn't prepared . . . .

To light a candle every year in place of going out to dinner,
seeing a play or planning a party. This summer
would have marked twenty-five years together.
Would we have gone dancing? A little circle

of light flickers on the ceiling, waltzing with the shadows.
I smile. You are dancing for me,
whirling in the endless light of memory.

Banquet Hall Collapse

In thirty seconds, a solid floor split,
and wedding guests plunged sixty feet.
The screams were caught on video
shown around the world on TV news.
I watched in horrid fascination:
they were dancing as they fell.

A smiling moment interrupted
by a floor's collapse—
it has happened in my life.
Since then, I don't stand
on any surface without suspicion.
Earthquakes could be waiting. . . .

That's why I need to dance.

ABOUT THE AUTHOR

Jacqueline Jules is the author of the poetry chapbook *Field Trip to the Museum*, published by Finishing Line Press, and two dozen books for young readers including the *Zapato Power series*, *No English*, *Sarah Laughs*, and *Never Say a Mean Word Again*. Her poetry has appeared in numerous publications including *Christian Science Monitor*, *Hospital Drive*, *Killing the Angel*, *Soundings Review*, *Third Wednesday*, *Inkwell*, *The Innisfree Poetry Journal*, *Imitation Fruit*, *Calyx*, *Connecticut River Review*, and *Pirene's Fountain*. She won the 2007 Arlington Arts Moving Words Contest, 2008 Best Original Poetry from the Catholic Press Association, 2009 SCBWI Magazine Merit Award for Poetry, and 2014 Spirit First Poetry Contest. Visit her online at www.jacquelinejules.com